LIVING FREE

―――― How to Stop Living Your Life ――――
According to Other People's
Expectations

Ashley Albers, DO

LIVING FREE: How to Stop Living Your Life According to Other People's Expectations

By: Ashley Albers, DO

ISBN for Print: 979-8-9909742-0-3

Copyright © 2024, Ashley Albers, DO

All rights reserved. No portion of this book may be reproduced in any form without permission from the author, except as permitted by U.S. copyright law.

For permissions, contact: ashley@rfscoaching.org

Cover design: Rhianon Paige

Editing: Dustin Dixon

Published by: AFGO Press

Printed in the United States

First Edition 2024

NOTICE: The information provided in this book is not to be construed as a substitute for medical advice or professional services of any kind. It is for educational purposes only. Neither the author nor the publisher make any representations or warranties, express or implied, about the accuracy, completeness, reliability, suitability, or availability with respect to the information, products, services, or related materials contained in this book for any purpose. The advice and strategies contained herein may not be suitable for your particular situation. Any use of this information is at your own risk.

For all those who have done it – who are living free.

You set the example of what is possible, and this world needs more people like you.

And for those still seeking their freedom, know that not only is it possible, it's yours for the taking.

Prepare to amaze yourself, and I can't wait to marvel at what you create.

TABLE OF CONTENTS

Introduction: Eaten Alive In One Bite — 11
The Living Free Framework — 19
    Step 1: UNCOVER — 33
    Step 2: ACCEPT — 39
    Step 3: OWN IT — 45
    Step 4: LIVE FREE — 53
The Fifth Step — 61
The End, But Not Really — 65
About the Author — 71
Acknowledgments — 75

A NOTE TO THE READER

Dear Reader,

As we begin, thank you for picking this book up and beginning the journey with me. This is the book I wish I'd had when I was at my lowest point, feeling not only stuck or trapped but caged in a prison from which there was no hope of escape. I have never been happier to be wrong, and I hope that if you are feeling trapped, you will read these words and know there is a way out.

You, too, can be free.

The **Living Free Framework** that I will be talking about is the product of my lived experience and my professional work as a coach and physician. Hospice doctor is still one of my favorite roles, and every patient I see teaches me how to live a good life and what freedom can mean.

I invite you to visit my website **www.livingfreeframework.com**, and take the **Living Free Quiz**. It's quick, easy, and will give you a clearer picture of what freedom means to you.

I trust that as you escape your cage and create the freedom you most desire, you will astound the world with what you do and who you become.

I can't wait to see it!

Ashley Albers
June 2024

INTRODUCTION

Eaten Alive In One Bite

I was heavily armored and battle-ready. Bracing myself as I headed for the building across the street, I tried to calm the storm that was swirling in my head.

No matter how hard I tried to prepare myself for these regularly scheduled meetings, nothing seemed to work.

Meeting with the boss tied me in knots before I even entered that beautifully decorated office.

As soon as I sat down, I would always set up my laptop to serve as a barrier between us. A pad of paper gave me a reason to avoid their gaze, although my well-honed *you-will-not-hurt-me-again* attitude fooled no one.

Both of us knew they could eat me alive in one bite.

Despite the big office, fancy title, and the perception that I had made it, I hated my job. I was certain it would eventually kill me (unless my boss got to me first).

I knew I wanted out. I was always journaling about needing to get out. But I just couldn't figure out how. Was it even possible that I could leave without making the rest of my life a whole lot worse?

As bad as it was, things didn't look any greener on the other side. When the COVID-19 pandemic hit, things got even darker. The hours got longer. We were under more scrutiny. There was suddenly no separation between work and home.

And yet… amid all that darkness, something suddenly occurred to me. I'd spent years believing that I could never successfully work from home. "I could never do *that*" was my mantra in those days.

That tiny flash of insight stayed with me. It explained why I had limited myself for decades. I allowed myself to stay stuck because of a mere belief that "I could never do *that*."

Whether it was working from home or doing one of a host of other things, the I-could-never-do-that belief would cost me countless career opportunities over the years.

But when the student is ready, the teacher appears, or so they say.

Now, I'm not exactly sure who or what represents the teacher in this scenario, but I suddenly found myself on the cusp of something big. I could feel myself getting closer to my "rock bottom." And I was determined to save myself before I got there.

‧

Eventually, I got the lesson, loud and clear: If I didn't take responsibility for every aspect of my life, not only my career and who I worked for but *all of it* – my relationships, my health, my finances – **I was destined to repeat the same negative cycles over and over and would NEVER be able to live the life I wanted.**

The realization of *that* hit me hard.

What made me think (and believe) that I had no power to design my life the way I wanted it?

What made me think I didn't have the power to make better choices? What made me think I couldn't tolerate other people's disappointment in me for making choices that I believed were in my best interests?

When did I lose myself?

How was I going to get myself back?

Rest assured, I took myself back in time, and in this book, I will show you how I did it with the hope of teaching you to do the same so that you, too, can begin to make choices that will allow you to *live free*.

‧

As a child, I could see where adult influencers and caregivers formed the foundation of a belief system that would run my life. It happens to all of us in varying degrees, and if we never confront the unconscious beliefs that no longer serve us in adulthood, we will stay locked in a cycle of perpetual "stuckness" that feels like we're locked in a cage with invisible bars and there appears to be no way out.

Think about it: as we grow up, we are indoctrinated into systems of beliefs about how the world works. Consider the "rules" that become part of those belief systems:

"Do as you're told."

"Be nice."

"You have to go to college."

"You should NEVER get divorced."

"It's always better to buy a house than to rent."

As children, we don't have much choice about what gets downloaded into our belief system, but as adults, we *can* choose to think and believe differently. After all, the choice isn't college vs. homeless, unemployed derelict. It's a false dichotomy. Life is so much more nuanced.

I realized that I had to be willing to re-evaluate anything and *everything* that I was taught, and some of it did not serve me. If we continue to believe that everything is black and white, just as we were taught, we accept that there are only two possible outcomes.

It wasn't until I was willing to question everything, even the people I'd always thought "knew best," that I finally understood I could have a say in my own life. More than that, to my great surprise, I could take charge of my life.

That feeling of being so completely stuck, certain that there was no right decision, is not something I would wish on anyone, even if that someone is The Inquisitor (my pet name for that boss I was telling you about). Too many people operate under the sunk cost fallacy that since they trained for a certain type of work or have been doing something for so long, they have to keep doing it.

They can't leave the job.

They can't leave the marriage.

They can't move to a new city!

They can't see what else might be out there because they don't understand how important it is to look at their core beliefs and determine what is true and right for them.

Until you are willing to take responsibility for every aspect of your life, you are allowing yourself to be pigeonholed into someone else's version of your life.

I lived that reality.

And until I was willing to make some significant changes – changes that had to occur on the inside of me – I would continue to miss out on how good life could be. My loved ones would miss out on having the real me, or at least a version of me who wasn't miserable. And the world would miss out on what I have to offer.

My life is a whole lot better since deciding to take responsibility for it, and when I surround myself with people who take full responsibility for their lives, things are even better. And that is too good not to share, hence, this book.

In the coming chapters, I'll introduce my **Living Free Framework** and how it was the impetus for my own personal transformation, one that dug me out of a hole that consisted of shame, blame, and anxiety on most days.

This is all optional, of course. Staying firmly ensconced in your comfort zone is one way to go. But I ask you, *at what cost?* Whatever it is that you're feeling, be it stuck, trapped, anxious, frustrated, angry, paralyzed, and/or miserable, it will not change unless you do.

It was a painful lesson for me to learn. I hope that I can make it less painful for you.

Whatever medications you may take or vacations you may go on to escape those feelings, they are like putting a small bandage on a deep wound.

It's hard to be present and feel delighted when you spend most of your time feeling anxious and trapped. I was missing out on my relationships, my health, and my ability to love the world around me.

"Delighted" was a feeling I barely understood. It wasn't even a feeling I thought I deserved.

As I began to understand my agency, I started seeing possibilities for myself. What if I didn't have to be miserable forever? That small hope that I might one day feel delighted led to more hope. I began to think that maybe, if this thing was possible, then maybe *that* thing could be too.

Like breadcrumbs, I followed the trail out of my darkness, and each small victory gave me the courage to dream even bigger. Sharing this process with you is a dream accomplished.

Let's see what we find when we dig up your dreams.

THE LIVING FREE FRAMEWORK

It was early in my relationship with one particular boss when I was asked my now least favorite question, "What's keeping you up at night?"

Thinking it was the right thing to do, I answered honestly.

It was most assuredly not the right thing to do.

I was immediately dismissed and shut down. We've all been there in one way or another. Most often, this shows up as the ubiquitous "How are you?" from a polite individual who doesn't care how you are. Social norms dictate that we answer "good" or "fine," and so we do. Change it to "great," and you will leave your questioner somewhat puzzled. Try "terrible" and watch them try to escape the conversation as quickly as possible. But this was not a chance encounter on the street.

So there I was, facing that now-hated question. I mistakenly thought that it was a real question and not just a box to check on the "meeting with the employee" agenda. (Imagine my surprise when I had direct reports and saw the official "meeting with the employee" forms!)

What was keeping me up at night, you see, was health-related and potentially life-altering, and I knew it. My life did change in both the short and long term. With the benefit of hindsight, I love where I am now, but I had no such certainty at that moment. But ultimately, it doesn't matter what it was. I could have named health concerns, relationship struggles, the state of the economy, or the health of the ozone layer, and I still would have been dismissed.

The response, "You'll be fine," left me feeling like I'd been hit by a truck. Being the smart and adaptable employee that I was, I quickly learned that there were only a few acceptable answers to that question, and while I never actually lost sleep over those things that were considered the "right answers," I never got that question wrong again.

I internalized a very important lesson on that fateful day: "I don't matter to this person that I work for."

It was neither my first opportunity to learn that lesson nor the last. But was it true? Ultimately, I don't know, and I cannot know. It is entirely possible that nobody was out to teach me a lesson that day, that the "lesson" is just a story I made up. Regardless, I do believe that organizations need employees who get the job done; that's why I've been hired for every job I've ever had, after all, but that doesn't answer the question of whether a boss cares about an employee or whether my boss cared about me. I chose to believe that mine didn't, and I acted in a way I thought would protect me.

For the duration of my time with that particular boss, I did not open up ever again, and I did not share anything that was not absolutely necessary. It was extreme, and while it felt like the right thing to do, it created some results that I really wasn't happy with, and I spent a long time playing the victim and blaming the whole thing on my boss.

It took me a while, but I learned to take radical responsibility for the way in which I communicate with my bosses. I am now very strategic in what I tell them and why, and as a result, I have been able to create collaborative relationships that support working well together.

Ultimately, as tempting as it is to want to blame others for all of the things that aren't perfect in life, that does not work. Not in business, not in relationships, not in anything. Yes, there are factors outside of our control. No, we cannot determine what other people will say or do. Even so, building the life you want is your responsibility.

If you do not choose to take responsibility for every aspect of your life, not only your career path, you will end up repeating the same negative cycles over and over and will never be able to live the life you want.

Even though there will be things outside your control, *you are the only person who can control your responses to the events around you*. You are the only person who has control of your thoughts and attitudes.

And when you take control of them, you begin to live *free*.

However, if you do not take responsibility for the way you think and how it affects your state of mind and, subsequently, the way you feel at any given moment, you will remain stuck in your current patterns. If those patterns negatively impact your life, you're likely to believe you're a victim of circumstance.

It is only when you choose to take responsibility for your thoughts, attitudes, responses, and every situation of your life that you will be able to build the life you desire.

This is what it means to live free. Free from the awful feelings associated with living your life according to the standards of someone else (and inevitably falling short). Free to make choices that are authentically yours and in your best interest.

Living free is what every person on this planet should get to do, and I've devised a strategy to make that happen.

In order to help guide you on the path to taking control of your life, I've created an easy-to-follow process called the **Living Free Framework**.

This framework, which I will detail below, is an answer to a very important question I suggest you ask yourself:

"What changes need to happen in my life so that I can feel happy and fulfilled – like I am living free?"

Take a moment to think about that.

Keep thinking.

Notice what your mind wants to tell you.

I can't do that… how will I pay my bills?

I'll let my parents/kids/partner/friends down if I do that. (Or, people depend on me. I can't let them down.)

I don't deserve something like that.

I've worked so hard to get where I am now; how can I just throw that all away?

I've been working at this job for so long that I wouldn't know how to do anything else.

That sounds amazing, but it isn't for people like me.

The old way of pursuing your career, picking one company to work for until you retire, believing that whatever you've trained for is the only thing you can do, trusting that if you just do your job well, it'll be easy to work your way up the ladder, rarely works.

It used to, that is certain. There was a time when loyalty to a company was both prized and rewarded, and a talented employee could expect to work their way into a managerial position with all the perks that came with that. Without the internet offering such a broad array of possibilities, it often didn't make sense to consider switching to a new career path as that might mean significant time and cost to retrain.

All of that has changed. Increasing numbers of people are discovering that they must move to a different company if they want a promotion. More than that, what someone wanted to do at age 20 might not be what they still want at 45, and there is a trend toward moving into a different industry or pursuing a different path altogether.

Sometimes this works. Some people make the big career shift and create a life they love. Others realize that they were, perhaps, too hasty to make a change and, therefore, seek a way to return to some version of their former role. Neither is universally right or wrong. It is ultimately a question of whether the decisions we make will create the life we want.

How, then, do we decide? And how do we make *responsible* decisions?

To begin taking responsibility for each area of your life, you must first understand how you got here. It requires becoming conscious and aware of the thoughts and beliefs that have created your current reality.

In order to "live free," you'll need to change some old habits. From there, you'll be better positioned to decide what you want your life to look like and how you will create that for yourself.

There is a degree of fluidity within the Living Free Framework; it's a 4-step process that will ebb and flow as you and the circumstances in your life change.

Here's how it works:

Step 1: Uncover

You will start by digging around to uncover your thoughts and beliefs. Whether they were imparted by the people who raised you or the influences of society as a whole, the important thing is that you understand what you believe now. In this process, you will also discover more about who you are and what it is that you want in this life.

This matters because, without this sort of awareness about how your mind works, you're flying blind. You are in reactive mode, with the circumstances of your life having more control over you than you have over them.

But when we uncover how our minds react to the circumstances of day-to-day living, we are in a better position to consciously choose to react in a way that is in our best interests.

Consider children who are raised in abusive households. Many grow up believing that the relationship patterns they witnessed are normal and go on to perpetuate them in their own relationships, often to their detriment. It is only when they become aware of those beliefs that they are able to make changes.

Similarly, when my dog was a very young puppy, I pushed the door to her crate shut but did not latch it. I called and called her, but she would not come because she believed she was locked in. As she grew and learned, she began to push at the door when I called her, and it opened immediately. Now, I push the door closed when it's in my way, and she comes out whenever she wants. (She likes it in there!)

When we uncover the secret world of our own mind and the thoughts we've been unaware of, we begin to free ourselves from much of the self-imposed suffering. We are surprised to find that there is a way out of that invisible cage we've locked ourselves in. With awareness, we can see what is keeping us stuck, and we can set ourselves free.

Step 2: Accept

After you uncover the thoughts and beliefs you didn't even know were allowed to roam free in your mind, the challenge is to accept what you cannot change. This allows you to stop fighting against an invisible enemy so that you can ultimately create the change you desire.

Byron Katie says, "When you argue with reality, you lose, but only 100% of the time." When we become aware of our thoughts and underlying beliefs, arguing and fighting to hold onto them is phenomenally tempting.

When I make my boss the villain, I also make myself a victim, powerless to do anything about the circumstances I'm in. It means I don't have to take any responsibility for changing, fixing, or doing something that would be better for me. Instead, I can blame it all on them.

The truth is, no matter the circumstances, I always have the power to decide *who I will be* in those circumstances – someone who is powerless to effect change or someone who is committed to standing up for herself in every aspect of her life. Painting someone as a villain doesn't let me off the hook when it comes to figuring out how to handle work (and life) situations that negatively impact me.

When we uncover our false beliefs about ourselves, we get closer to the truth of who we really are – not a victim, but someone who uncovers her false beliefs and… creates something amazing.

It's how I became the heroine in my own story.

Step 3: Own It

We each have a remarkable amount of control over our lives, but too often, we abdicate that control and give our power to others.

Rather than allowing others to "make" you feel a certain way, you can take responsibility for how you want to react.

Own it all.

This allows you to begin creating the life you want now, regardless of whether you choose to change your circumstances.

The power you have to control your thoughts and reactions and create a different outcome for your life cannot be overstated.

Consider the example of getting cut off in traffic. I have been known to make up stories about how terribly incompetent and horrible some drivers are and how they ought not to be driving at all, and I've gotten quite mad about it. I've also taken a gentler approach and wondered whether they're hurrying because there's an emergency and they must get to the hospital. That curiosity brings up an entirely different set of feelings in me.

While that's a simple example, it illustrates the power of taking responsibility for our own responses and feelings. The driver of the other car doesn't "make" me angry or sympathetic; my stories about the driver cause that. That is true in so many situations in life, and owning responsibility for our feelings will change the experiences we have in every aspect of our lives.

Step 4: Live Free!

Once you learn how to take back control over the way you tend to think and react to the people and things that happen in your life, you begin to see a whole new world open up to you. You now get to design the life you actually *want*.

Real and lasting change is finally possible as you now understand why things worked out the way they did in the past. Knowing what to do now, you'll be amazed at your results.

℘

Do you know what you want? Quite often, we know what we *don't* want but don't take the time to decide what we *do* want.

I don't want to feel stuck.

I don't want to work for this boss forever.

I don't want to be single anymore.

Or, *I don't want to be in this relationship anymore.*

Can you see how repeating those words only serves to perpetuate a culture of remaining stuck?

And yet, that is where we focus so much of our time and attention.

Focusing on what we don't want or wishing for things to be different only gets us more of what we don't want because we are limited in our ability to contemplate other options. Even more, it limits our ability to make progress toward the things we do want.

"I don't want to work for this boss anymore" places all the focus on the current boss and how miserable it feels to work for them.

Even though I couldn't change my boss, taking responsibility for how I could change myself made life less miserable. Instead, I could muster the resolve to find a work environment that would be collaborative and in which I would have a boss who supports me. Taking responsibility to make this happen was so much better than feeling "hopeless."

Uncovering your beliefs is a journey of self-discovery that usually does not follow a clear, linear path. You may first decide what you want to see change and how you want life to look, and then go in search of the beliefs and expectations that are keeping you stuck. Deciding what you want *without examining your beliefs* will likely land you back where you were.

This work is not for the faint of heart. Journeying into your mind to understand yourself better is hard work and takes a commitment to change because you are no longer willing to meet the expectations others have for you.

Be prepared because it can dramatically change the dimensions of all your relationships.

If you're not satisfied with your life, or if you want something more, my Living Free Framework will guide you there. When you wake up feeling stuck and trapped at work, worried that nothing will ever change, the only decision you need to make right now is to take everything I'm proposing to you into consideration.

Because you are correct: nothing will change unless and until you are willing to take the steps to change it. But take heart because as difficult or impossible as this may feel or sound, it is immensely rewarding, and the life you want is closer than you think.

Change is hard. Undoubtedly, you have experienced the truth in that, and it is worth reminding yourself that you have changed before, you survived it, and many times it was better in the end.

It takes courage to question an old belief and decide to believe something new.

It took months of practice to believe that I did not have to armor up for battle to go meet with my boss. I could have continued to steel myself each time, but had I done that, I would still believe those meetings were a battlefield that felt "dangerous" to me. It took courage to question my old beliefs and even more courage to show up and act differently.

But first, I had to try a new way of thinking about my boss. One I could actually believe. For example, it would be futile to try to tell myself, "I can handle *this* boss," because I wasn't sure I could. But I could believe that the actions of my boss had nothing to do with me and that their behaviors were a reflection of their own beliefs and mental capacity.

It worked.

The first step is being willing to consider that what you "know" to be true might not actually be true. When you are willing to get curious about what you believe and how your beliefs are creating the results that you are getting in your work and life, you are ready to begin this journey of self-discovery.

My willingness to dive in and to understand the twists and turns of my thoughts and beliefs set off the chain reaction to building the life I want. As I continue to do this work, I get closer each day, and I am so excited for you to learn more in the next chapters.

STEP ONE

Uncover

One day, in a session with my first coach, I recounted an interaction I had recently had with my boss. They very gently showed me how my response in that interaction was not as useful as I had thought it was.

During a conversation with that particular boss, I became quite reactive, and my response to something my boss said ended the conversation rather abruptly. My words felt true in the moment, but saying them out loud did not serve anyone. I thought I was speaking the truth, but my coach helped me to see that I was responding to a story in my head. Only with that awareness could I begin to choose my responses.

That's the challenge, and "challenge" is probably an understatement.

We talk about awareness in other situations. A person who is not aware of their surroundings when crossing the street is likely to end up in an accident. My lack of awareness of what my mind was thinking meant I was actually making some situations worse.

I was powerless to fix those situations because I could not uncover the root of the problem and my part in it. Becoming aware is the first step towards living free, and until you take that step, you will remain stuck in a life you don't want.

To be clear, we all do this and in more ways than one. I can look back now and see that it wasn't just that one relationship that was impacted by my lack of awareness. I struggled in so many areas of my life and in so many relationships because I simply could not see.

That's what a lack of awareness does: it keeps us struggling and stuck. So then we can't see a way out, we can't see our options, and we believe nothing will ever change.

Uncovering the thoughts and beliefs that run our lives can reveal several areas. By uncovering the underlying beliefs that don't serve us, we are able to make permanent changes.

I did struggle to resist the habit of armoring up for meetings with my new boss. But when I changed jobs, things were different. And this time, I was different.

I was working for a completely different person, in a completely different organization, and in a completely different company culture. That sounds like a good thing, and it was. But if I had not changed, if I had entered my new job with my old thought habits and beliefs, I would have found a way to repeat the same old patterns.

Instead, as my new self, I was able to approach the situation differently and with greater curiosity.

Because I now had an awareness of what was going on inside of me, I could show up differently; I could explore my new situation and craft a strong and collaborative relationship with my new boss. While I no longer work for them, I still consider them to be a kind and willing resource whom I would not hesitate to contact if I needed assistance. But had I lacked that awareness, I would have remained closed off and mistrustful and would probably still consider every boss to be a source of danger.

Let me reiterate. Because I became aware of my underlying beliefs about bosses and meetings with bosses (they're bad, scary, unhelpful, and "you'd better armor up"), I was able to challenge my thinking and, therefore, change the relationship I've had with every boss since. It wasn't easy, but it was absolutely worth it.

We see it in other areas of our lives, too. When people become aware of the thoughts and beliefs that are holding them back or keeping them stuck, things they thought were impossible begin to happen. Weight is lost. Marathons are run. Cross-country (or international) moves happen. Businesses are started. Jobs and promotions are applied for. Jobs are left.

All because people become aware of the beliefs that are holding them back and choose to take the next steps to make lasting change.

I've seen it happen time and again with my clients.

And it can happen to you, too, dear reader.

If you aren't living the life you want, it doesn't mean that that life is impossible. It means you haven't taken responsibility for creating the freedom you seek, and the first step toward that is to uncover the beliefs that are holding you back.

Without awareness, any attempt to obtain the life you want will fail, and this happens for a few reasons. The first is that you cannot have the life you want unless and until you know what you want. Then, you have to uncover the reasons why you don't yet have it.

I spent a lot of time believing that I just wanted a relationship with a boss who I wasn't afraid of. Now, as I have gained greater awareness of what I believe and what is possible in the world, I know that I want one who is supportive, available, and willing to listen. I am also willing to speak up and ask for what I want and need, which comes from being aware of my beliefs and habits.

Uncovering how your thoughts and beliefs hold you back is a step that is almost always overlooked. There is a tendency to focus on changing our behavior without addressing what drives the behavior.

You simply cannot create the life you most desire if you continue to believe the thoughts that are keeping you in the life you have now.

Having a coach point out my reactivity was a hard lesson as I began to realize that I might not be as "right" as I thought I was. It was challenging to look back and see that I hadn't asked for what I needed and how my stories kept me stuck. It was when I became aware that I was telling stories that *might* not be true that I could start taking steps to move forward to get the life I wanted.

This is the reward of uncovering the inner workings of our mind. Without this awareness, you stay stuck, repeating the same cycles of beliefs and actions that got you exactly where you are now.

With the clarity that awareness brings, you're now ready to take the next step. While awareness of all the ways you hold yourself back is necessary, seeing what is possible can feel expansive and open and make you feel a pull to move forward.

So, what do you say?

Ready for the next step?

STEP TWO

Accept

Can you accept the things in your life you don't have the power to change?

Can you accept that it is futile to argue with what happened in the past?

Uncovering the way our mind thinks and then accepting only what *cannot* be changed is how we create freedom.

It is vital that acceptance follows awareness because we cannot change what has already been. If I have been thinking thoughts that serve only to keep me stuck, I can choose to learn to think something different, but I cannot change the days or years that I have spent thinking those things.

That is, perhaps, the most difficult part of making changes in our lives. It's called the sunk cost fallacy. We imagine that because we've already spent so much time or money on something, starting over would be like throwing it all away.

But that isn't true.

You're never starting over from nothing. You're starting over from experience.

So, dear reader, if you find yourself thinking that this process seems like throwing it all away, please consider the fact that, at the very least, you know now what you *don't* want.

This process is about figuring out what you do want so that you can go get it and finally begin to live free.

There are two forms of acceptance we can choose, and only one is really useful to our cause. One option is to admit that something happened and then shove it aside and move on.

It doesn't work. I've tried it.

I worked for a boss who was unavailable and (I thought) rather unhelpful. They did not show up for scheduled one-to-one meetings and repeated the "we have to do more with less" mantra. At the time, it felt easier to grit my teeth and move on with my day, but I see now how harmful that was for me.

The other option, the more useful option, is acceptance with deep feeling and processing. This would have been much better for my long-term mental and emotional health, not to mention getting really clear on what I wanted and what I would and would not tolerate if I had taken the time to *feel* my anger. Their decision to no-show meant wasting the time I spent waiting for them, disrupted my day, and caused my attempts to do the "more" that they wanted to take up so much more of my precious evening time. Anger would have been an appropriate response rather than the resigned forward motion that I chose.

This is hard. I don't particularly enjoy feeling angry, and it's natural to try to avoid feeling hard emotions. But feeling the hard emotions and processing the feelings that come with the thing we've recently become aware of is how we take responsibility for our lives.

The truth is that my boss skipped meetings and said words. It's as simple as that. I cannot change those facts, and it would be a waste of time and energy to try. What I can do is become aware of the thoughts and feelings I have about that situation. I absolutely developed a few new beliefs as a result of what happened.

Some of those new beliefs included things like "there's no point in asking for help since it will never come."

"I'm not worth my boss's time."

"I'm working myself to death trying to get it all done."

Have you ever felt this? Whether about a workplace situation or a personal relationship in your life?

I'm sure you have.

If you're like me, those thoughts led you down a dangerous path toward overwork and burnout.

Do you hear the blame in those opinions? It sounds like it was clearly the fault of the person and the system that I felt the way I did. But that wasn't true, and if I could go back and change the narrative, I would.

For example, instead of, "I'm not worth my boss's time" to ask for help, I could have changed the thought to, "It's worth *my* time to ask for help." If I held that belief about myself, the outcome would have surely been much different.

But that time has passed, and I am now left with a choice: I can beat myself up over it and wish that I had reacted and believed differently, or I can accept that those are the things I chose to believe at the time. Beating myself up now will only lead to more bruises and misery. Acceptance is not easy, but it affords me the opportunity to learn from what happened and choose a different future. So I chose to believe that my past self was doing the best she could with the resources she had and decided that I no longer have to believe those things.

Easier said than done, right? Making peace with the past so that it doesn't interfere with the future is one of humanity's greatest challenges.

It's not supposed to be easy. But, I think we can all see that it is worth our effort.

Accepting what has been and what "is" opens up the possibility for change. When we are expending our energy resisting things, we don't have that energy available to make changes in our lives. When we choose to accept what was and move on, we can use that situation as a powerful educational opportunity. We then get to choose how we want to understand the situation, what we want to believe about our work and ourselves, and how we want to treat any future employees we may have.

Before choosing to get very curious and move into deep acceptance, I allowed those outside influences to keep me from creating the life that I wanted. I was experiencing the natural consequences of my thoughts and beliefs and found myself operating from a place of scarcity and a lack of control.

That's the danger if we decide not to move into acceptance. Without acceptance, we can feel as though we are at the mercy of whatever is happening outside us, and from there, it is very easy to begin to feel completely stuck. When we're stuck, we often feel stressed, anxious, and hopeless. We're not able to see opportunities to learn and grow, and the life we actually want never seems to materialize.

These are hard consequences, and I have spent more time living them than I really want to admit. But that is what happened, and I get to choose to accept that, too.

I suspect that if you're reading this book, you know what I'm describing.

You, too, have the ability to embrace those circumstances and accept them for everything that they've taught you.

That is why this is the necessary second step in the Living Free Framework.

Without it, we couldn't possibly move toward the future that we desire because we will continue to remain in and resent the past.

No matter what you might think, you do not deserve to live there forever. Allow yourself a little grace as you move through these pages.

Once we become aware of the thoughts and beliefs that are holding us back or remember the circumstances that led to the creation of those beliefs, deep acceptance is the necessary step in moving forward. Only when we are willing to process our feelings about what has happened can we take back control of our lives and begin to create the life we want.

To be clear, acceptance does not mean agreeing that what happened was ok or condoning a harmful or illegal event. It is possible to believe that something was absolutely wrong and still accept that it happened and the thoughts and feelings that you have about it.

Your life is more than what has happened to you.

Your future can be whatever you want it to be, especially if you take responsibility for making it happen.

In Step 3, we will learn why the only person (or thing) that can give you the life you want is you.

It's time to move out of the shadow of your past and toward that bright future. One step at a time.

STEP THREE

Own It

One of the best pieces of life advice I have ever received came from a senior resident when I was an intern doing an ICU rotation. "Run the unit," they said, "or it will run you."

I thought I understood. I thought they were only talking about the ICU. Perhaps that was the case, but it turns out that this applies to life in general.

Run your life? It sounds kind of obvious, doesn't it?

But how often do we find ourselves running breathlessly between tasks until we feel like we're drowning?

When I allow my life to run me, I find myself overwhelmed by the sheer volume of stuff that there is to do and manage. The job, the house, the yard, the relationships, the wants, the projects, the chores just all seem to be too much. It doesn't take long to be spinning in anxiety, wondering how in the world others seem to get it all done.

That's what it *looks* like. The mythical "others" get it all done. There are those who homeschool and run businesses and travel and hike and seem to have it all. I want to ask them how they do it.

The short answer is that they run their lives instead of letting their lives run them.

Running your life goes hand in hand with owning it because when you own your life and everything in it, you take responsibility for its wellbeing.

This means that you understand that the only person who can run your life is you.

When I own my life, I feel better. I trade overwhelm and anxiety for calm, confidence, strength, and determination. Why? Because when I own my life, I become the person who can feel those things no matter what is going on around me.

That's the secret. It isn't about knowing what to do or having a magic formula to make it all ok. In that ICU, there was no way to plan the day and expect that we could use the same formula day in and day out and expect the unit to behave itself. Nor can we expect that what we do in life today will work exactly the same as yesterday or tomorrow.

In short, "owning your life" means taking responsibility for it.

For all of it. The good and the bad.

When you don't, it's overwhelming at best. You are likely to find that you are at the mercy of everyone else's priorities and to-dos, and your own desires take a backseat.

The truth is that that's even an understatement. For a long time, my desires and priorities didn't take a backseat because they never even made it on the bus. Depending on the family you were raised in, the career you chose, and the voices you heard while you were growing up, you were taught to put the needs of others above your own. To serve, no matter what it cost you.

And, I'm sorry to say, it did cost you. And me.

When your wants, your desires, take the backseat, you miss out on so much. Your autonomy and freedom. Your ability to make the decisions that best serve *you*. The future that is possible if you'll only reach out and take it.

When you think about it in those terms, it hurts. It's like a knife to the heart in a way that we don't often allow ourselves to feel. When you don't take responsibility and don't own your life, you miss out on what is possible for you.

What could be if you only reached out to take it?

We can go big and say that the world misses out when you aren't all that you could be. While there is value in that, it isn't enough. It's actually the problem. It's in doing and attempting to be everything that the world around us wants that we lose control. Reclaiming responsibility for running our lives is a revolutionary act. That is why it's so important. Without it, we are, at best, cogs in the machine. With it, at a minimum, we change the world.

If you want to live free, you have to take responsibility for the only thing in this world that you can control.

That's right, it's you.

If that sounds like an exaggeration, think again. Consider the people you know who are the most responsible for their own lives. They seem strangely magnetic, as though there is something they have that you want, and being around them gives you both a sense of what is possible for you and of the changes you would need to make to get there.

People who own their lives create a sort of gravitational shift that impacts everyone and everything around them. Whatever it is that you want to accomplish in this world, that is how you make it happen.

The challenge is that most of us are walking around and living in resentment or so much stress that we cannot possibly be our best selves.

People who own their lives shine differently.

They speak differently.

They move differently.

They live free, and everyone around them can see it.

They are delight-*full*.

In a prior job, I thought the most important thing I needed to do was whatever someone else said, and I let that spill over until it ran my life. I was answering emails at all hours of the day and night and worked every weekend for entirely too long.

I felt completely out of control.

While I wasn't happy, the serious unraveling began when I was asked to do something for a family member. I didn't understand their deadline and didn't have the bandwidth to ask. So, instead of honoring their request, which is actually what I wanted to do, I let my job stay in control and missed the opportunity. They assumed one thing. I felt terrible. It wasn't the experience any of us wanted.

Let me say that again.

Before I learned to take responsibility for my life, I believed that I was at the mercy of my employers, doomed to follow their every whim. It worked for a while, as there are expectations that we all must meet to complete medical training. But while it was one thing to believe that my program directors knew more about being a good doctor than I did, it was quite another to believe that my boss knew more than I did about *my life* and what it should look like.

Believing that made it easy to blame them for everything. The number of hours I was working, the ongoing frustrations with my work, and my inability to show up for the people I care about the most.

The hard truth is that it was my decision, my stories, and my lack of responsibility that led to that failure.

You might think that that is a hard thing for me to admit. But, after working with the Living Free Framework for so long, I recognize it as the vehicle of change in my life.

And it could be the same for you.

So there it was, staring me in the face: the life I DIDN'T want. The life I wanted required me to take responsibility for creating it. When I didn't do that, I ended up in a situation that I did not want. Every time I relinquish my autonomy and responsibility, it has landed me squarely in a life I don't want.

But here's the caveat: if I had skipped awareness and acceptance and gone straight to responsibility, it would have backfired.

In that scenario, family would have replaced work, and I would eventually end up resenting the ones I love the most.

"Owning" the responsibility for creating the freedom we seek can only come when we truly understand who we are, what we think, and what we want, and when we have come to a deep acceptance of all of these. Without the first two steps, we trade one master for another and never actually take responsibility for the lives we want. It may look like we do at first, but we quickly realize that we are trapped again.

It is equally dangerous to skip this step!

It is extremely tempting to say, "I know what I want, I've made peace with the past, and I'm ready to claim my future!" without understanding what that means. I highly recommend going forth and claiming your future, but it isn't actually that simple, though it would be nice if it were.

Claiming your future and taking responsibility for your life requires difficult choices. This may mean saying an outright "No" to someone or something that demands your time, energy, or attention, but it may also mean choosing between two opposing priorities.

It becomes even more interesting and challenging when we find ourselves caught between something promising an immediate benefit and something promising a long-term benefit. Those are often extraordinarily difficult choices, and it takes courage to choose the one that will most benefit you.

When it feels as though the world is pulling you in a multitude of directions, one of the hardest things is to say No *on purpose* so that you can choose what you most want or what will lead you to the life you don't want. It's also one of the most important things.

Without it, you will likely find yourself adrift and buffeted by the forces that all want something from you. Where you end up seems like it is up to them.

I'm here to tell you that even if your boat is slowly sinking, you're still the captain of that vessel, and you can sail it in any direction you want.

Into the storm or out of it?

But when you are willing to step up and run your own life, to take responsibility for all parts of it, then you will be able to choose wisely and create the life you most desire.

What is that life you most desire? What would you be willing to do to have it? We know that obtaining it isn't easy, but it is possible.

Once you understand that this life is what you make it and believe that in your bones, you will finally be able to make it into whatever you want.

You will finally be able to take meaningful action in that direction.

You'll be ready to start living free.

STEP FOUR

Live Free

Looking back on it, I can see now that the biggest cause of my suffering was that I was living in a way that was not in alignment with my values.

As I made the change, I did some very intentional soul-searching and realized just how far off track I'd gotten.

I wasn't showing up for the people and things I cared most about and I hated myself for not being the person I wished to be. Getting out of that and taking action to become the person I want to be and create the life that I want took a lot of work.

But as hard as it was, it is so much better than living out of alignment and feeling trapped.

Step 4 is where you finally begin to take meaningful action toward the things that you want in life and *living free*.

That means authentically, intentionally, and unapologetically showing up for yourself, day in and day out. Every day, you will be faced with choices and situations. Some may cause fear, doubt, or any other mix of emotions that used to make you feel stuck or like you didn't have a choice.

But, once you've gone through the Living Free Framework and arrived at this step, you will be fully equipped to face these situations with a newfound sense of purpose and self.

You will finally understand what it means to live free.

When we're feeling stuck, being told that the possibilities are endless can feel insulting or like an outright lie. But when you are aware of your thoughts and the limitations they impose on you, you can begin to see the wide range of options that you have.

I spent years believing that I could NEVER work from home and had a lengthy list of reasons to back that belief up. Those reasons, of course, were just stories I kept telling myself. The COVID-19 pandemic forced my hand when my company moved to remote work, and I was suddenly working from home.

Not only did I discover that I *could* work remotely, I *loved* working remotely. Changing my old beliefs opened up a world of possibilities and led to me applying for the remote job that I now have.

I spent a lot of time believing that the life I had was one that I was stuck with. More than stuck, I felt despair. Of course, I did. Telling myself stories about how it is going to be this way forever doesn't produce very many positive emotions. Taking action from that place was doomed to fail; I couldn't change my state of being without first understanding the stories I was telling.

That is why Step 4 must come at the end of the Living Free Framework. Becoming aware, finding that deep acceptance, and then deciding to take responsibility was necessary in order to make any lasting change.

The challenge is that nobody can do it for you. The good news is that it's entirely up to you. This is where taking responsibility for every part of your life comes into play.

When you let someone else be in control, you end up following some version of their path, and it often isn't long before you're out of alignment with your values and wondering how you got to where you are and why your life is the way it is.

But when you take responsibility, you become the person who chooses the path, and you can choose to stay in alignment with what you value most.

Now that you have an awareness of your thoughts and beliefs, deep acceptance of what is and what has been, and understand the need to take responsibility for your own life, you get to take action.

This is action that will produce lasting results because it comes from a place of deep understanding and acceptance, and it is based on your own values. Too often, we try to take action based on what others tell us to do, abdicating our own responsibility, and of course, it doesn't last.

Speaking of taking action, let's talk a little about the mindset that is required.

Ultimately, this is always mindset first, action second. The mindset that has gotten you the life you have now will only serve to get you more of the same. But you want something different, and so your mindset has to shift.

The good news is that it already has.

By gaining awareness, choosing acceptance, and taking responsibility for your life, you have a different mindset. You are now ready to approach your life not as a victim, but as the master of your own destiny. The captain of your own ship, if you will.

The captain of the ship is actually a perfect metaphor. If you point a ship at its destination and then do nothing further, it's hard to say where you'll end up. Wind and waves play a role and the captain must correct for these factors if they ever hope to make it to their destination.

Likewise, you will face your own form of wind and waves that will attempt to push you off course. These challenges come in many forms and are often what we blame for not being where we want to be. It's the fault of the boss, or the political climate, or the markets, or whatever other source we could find to blame.

But no more.

In your new mindset, you do not play the victim.

The obstacles can be whatever they are, but your level of self-responsibility means that you get to choose your response to them and decide how you choose to proceed. You get to decide that this will not stop you from reaching your goal.

Your mindset, then, is one of fierce determination.

This is a remarkable place to be in. You will find yourself moving ever closer to your goal. Better still, this usually isn't an all-or-nothing proposition. Most likely, the life you most want isn't something that you either have or don't have. Many of these things are a continuum, so you'll find yourself enjoying what you want even while you work to make it better or to get more of it.

It would be lovely to simply jump into claiming the life you want, wouldn't it? But we know now that it doesn't work, and really, most of us have tried it.

Without the understanding and **awareness** of what it is that we really believe, without truly understanding who we are, what we want, and why we don't have it yet, we can't have it. It all starts there. Moving through **acceptance** and **responsibility** is also necessary to put you in a position to finally claim the life you want.

Remember that this is a process. If the road ahead looks daunting, I would invite you to turn around and look behind you. The fact that you have read this far means that you are well on the path to the life you want. That progress is something to celebrate and proof that the life you want is within reach.

In my own journey, not showing up for my family was one of my biggest failures and one of the most impactful drivers in how I have created my life now. If I say that I value my family but continue not to show up for them, I am living well outside of my integrity, and I am not willing to do that. Most of us want to live in integrity with our values.

What values are important to you?

How do you want to show up in your life? Not only for yourself but for the people and things that you care about.

What does living free really mean to you?

One way that shows up in my life now is in my work schedule. I am often asked to work weekends, and I am happy to accept most of the time. I do not work out of town on important holidays because I spend those with my family, and I try to avoid working on birthdays. Yes, I do occasionally end up working on a day that we want to celebrate, but those times are the exceptions, not the rule. I also don't work on my birthday simply because I value having that day off.

That is but one example. Living in integrity with your values and claiming the life you want looks different for every person. You could try to follow my blueprint, and some things might be better, but ultimately, that would abdicate your responsibility and leave you in the same position you have been in before, responding to the whims and desires of everyone else around you.

So it is vital that you claim the life you want, not the life someone else wants from you.

Owning your life and learning to live in integrity with your values is not easy. For one thing, there are other humans involved, and they may have needs and expectations of you, too. Whether it's your boss expecting a certain behavior or work schedule or a partner or child needing things from you at home, you likely face demands and expectations from others. Really, everything from our finances to our families can seem to get in the way of crafting the ideal life.

But this is a journey that gets better as we move along. Will you have your ideal life while your kids are toddlers or while you work for this particular boss? Perhaps not, but you can choose how you will respond to these circumstances and what you might do to change them. Most importantly, you choose your responses, thoughts, and beliefs. Daunting as it may seem, it's all figureoutable, and figuring out how to create the life you want, even within your current constraints, is the most magical thing of all.

So there you have it: the life you want. Or at least, you know now what that life could look like.

Are you ready to start making your way there, one step at a time?

Once you have done the work to understand where you are and the thoughts and beliefs that got you there, accepted where you are, and chosen to take responsibility for your life, you finally get to claim the life you want. You get to decide what it is that you value most and figure out how to live in integrity with that. It is both simple and daunting. It can be quite challenging to figure these things out, particularly when they seem to contradict each other. But each time you do, you bring yourself more and more into the life you most want.

As you figure each piece out, your skill at creating the life you want grows. It gets easier to examine where you are and understand what's holding you back. Eventually, you can see your own blind spots.

Until then, and in my experience *even* then, it's helpful to have a coach to guide you through the process. There is nothing quite like the breakthrough and rapid change that comes when a caring guide helps you see what's holding you back and helps you figure out what to change.

Now it's time. You have the awareness, the acceptance, the willingness to take responsibility, and the opportunity to claim the life you want.

Now, dear reader, it's time to discover what steps you can take in this moment to begin to live free.

THE FIFTH STEP

Surely, you know by now that the life you want *is* possible.

You know that it's possible because you're watching someone else live it. You're sitting there eyeing them, wishing you could have what they have.

You may be worrying that it's possible for everyone else but you, afraid that if you go after it, if you want it too much, you'll just end up more disappointed than before.

Afraid that this life that you have now really is all there is.

Maybe you're worried that you'll get there and discover that it isn't everything you thought it was.

But you know what? Those are all just beliefs couched in worry. They are simply stories that you tell yourself that keep you exactly where you are now.

Hey, wait, did you just develop an awareness of one of your beliefs? (Getting started is actually that simple.)

Now that you've read this far, you have options.

Option 1: Embrace the status quo and do nothing.

What we call the comfort zone is a tempting place. While you may not be entirely comfortable there, sticking with "the devil you know" is sometimes safer. I've certainly done it. I've allowed the fear of what it would mean to change to keep me stuck in a place of misery.

Maintaining the status quo may seem easier than examining your thoughts and beliefs. In the short term, it can be hard to do the work to uncover your beliefs and take responsibility for your life. It may even seem scary. But I wonder what is more frightening, to uncover your beliefs or one day wish that you had done this work?

Option 2: Decide to change and go it alone.

There are many ways of capturing your thoughts and figuring out what beliefs are holding you back. You have the steps, and you can begin to implement them and make changes.

I think back to that day with my first coach, who pointed out how reactive I was and how that wasn't serving me. It's possible that I would have figured that out on my own, but I can guarantee it wouldn't have happened that day or even that year!

In any great adventure story, the hero has companions, mentors, and guides who share their wisdom and personal experiences.

Without them, there's a good chance the hero's journey takes him back to where he started. In other words, change is usually temporary.

Option 3: Decide to get help.

There is no shame in getting help and no badge of honor for going it alone, although it is tempting to think that we should be able to pull ourselves up by our proverbial bootstraps and make it all work out. But why? When there are others who have walked the path before us, why would we choose to go it alone?

One of my biggest lessons was that I didn't know my mind as well as I thought it did. But with the help of my coaches, I was able to uncover thoughts and beliefs that were buried so deep it's not likely I would ever have found them.

Having someone who can help you see how your thoughts and beliefs are holding you back is nothing short of eye-opening.

☙

The steps we've talked about in this book are only the beginning. The next logical step, or what I call "the fifth step," is a biggie: What will you do after you close this book?

Will you tell yourself, "Well, that was interesting." and do nothing? Or will you finally decide to take a step towards living free?

If you'd like to discuss your options, I invite you to visit my website www.livingfreeframework.com, where you'll find more information about what it might look like to work together. If nothing else, you'll have an opportunity to take the **Living Free Quiz.** I'm certain you will be surprised by the insight you'll receive simply by answering a few yes/no questions.

Whatever option you choose now, know that I've been there. I've (unconsciously) chosen to stay stuck because I thought the status quo was my only option.

I also tried to change things in my life by reading some books and doing it myself. Not surprisingly, that never got me very far.

It wasn't until I decided I needed the guidance of someone who'd already walked in my shoes that my life changed in ways I never would have believed possible.

My hope for you is that you will have everything you need to choose to craft the life you want on *purpose*.

But first, you'll need to take a conscious step toward freedom.

I can't wait to see where that takes you!

THE END, BUT NOT REALLY

I've told the story of my transformation enough times that I can now tell it in just a couple of sentences and make it sound remarkably simple. While part of me wishes it was, I wouldn't have become the person I am now if it were that easy. Re-writing the stories I used to tell about my work, myself, my life, and other people has been a challenging and ongoing process. I liken it to peeling an onion – just when I think I've taken care of something, there's another layer underneath.

That's a good thing. As I work through each layer, I uncover and shed more limiting beliefs and step ever closer to the person I was meant to be, to the person I am at my core, without all the baggage that I've picked up along the way.

In short, I become more free with each layer of self-imposed suffering I manage to peel away.

I've always loved the idea of magic and the instant transformations it can provide. Think about the prince becoming the beast and then becoming the prince again. That's the magic we're going for.

Except it's not really magic – it's insight.

Young children have wide-open imaginations with every possibility under the sun available to them. Personally, I wanted to be everything from an astronaut to a librarian when I grew up, and I ended up doing neither, which demonstrates that there is so much more available to us than we can imagine at any one point in time.

What's most important is that I learned how to *be* myself.

Through this work, you will uncover who you are at your deepest level and unleash a universe of possibilities. Yes, you read that right. Your options broaden with every layer you peel away.

I went gem mining with a friend not too long ago. We knew roughly what would be in the bucket, but it was still fun to pan through and see what we could find, but then we had to ask for help identifying it!

I tend to gloss over the part of my story that involves burnout and quickly move on to being the heroine who got what she wanted. But if it had been that easy, I wouldn't be where I am today, sharing my story with you. Instead, I took the time and did the work to uncover the beliefs that were the source of so much of my suffering. During that process, I unearthed entire belief systems that dictated my identity, my self-worth, my perceived place in the world, and more.

When I began doing this work for myself, I was already in the midst of a significant career change. It was born out of sheer desperation, and I promised myself that my new job was allowed to be temporary so I could "figure out" what I actually wanted to do next.

Instead, I learned that it was never about the job. I uncovered stories about how much of myself I needed to give to *my job* in order to be considered "good."

When I learned to own my life, I took control of the definitions, too. Now, if I want to call myself "good," I base it on a definition of my own choosing rather than on what anyone else says.

I gloss over my burnout story in part because an honest telling might get very confusing.

I was working for this company and telling myself a story that I had to be ALWAYS ON and could NEVER have a real vacation because I always had to be reachable, and, of course, I got calls on vacation and emails at all hours of the night. So I could never rest, and I had to do all the things because…

I feel anxious just writing that! Telling myself I had to be "always on" and never going on vacation kept me feeling painfully trapped in my own life.

But they were just stories.

As so many stories do, they had enough reality in them to appear to be perfectly true. There is a paper trail that proves that I received phone calls from my employer while on vacation and that one individual sent emails until 11 pm while another began sending them around 3 am!

Today, I clearly see what I could not see back then. I did not "have to" respond to emails at 3 am, but believing that I was "always on" made sure that I did.

The need to be good was powerful... until I didn't need it anymore.

Uncovering the beliefs I hold and the stories I tell myself is an ongoing process. Some of those stories I'm happy to continue to hold on to because they are helping me get to where I want to go. There are others, however, that can't go away quickly enough (Good riddance, I tell them).

And there are still others that I continue to fight with, struggling both to accept what I have believed and to take ownership and change it. What's different is that I'm able to see how I am the cause of the struggle. I don't need to blame anyone else. As I strive to tell better stories, I take comfort in knowing that I always have the power to create the freedom I seek.

When I look back, I couldn't have imagined the life that I have now and the ways I get to feel. I look forward, too, to the things I want and wonder what's to come that I can't yet imagine.

And yes, I practice what I preach, and I'll be seeing my coach just a few hours after writing these words.

That's the beauty of the journey – you always have the ability to step back, re-evaluate, and continue to grow throughout the rest of your life.

What could be more exciting than that?

ABOUT THE AUTHOR

Ashley Albers is a doctor of osteopathic medicine (DO). After completing her medical training, Ashley spent the early part of her career working in end-of-life care. She will happily share the lessons that she has learned and is still learning from her patients and coworkers.

Since experiencing burnout, Ashley has done the work first to see and then change her thoughts to live the life she *wants*. Now, after experiencing what it means to "live free," she coaches others so they, too, can experience the lives they most desire. Seeing their eyes light up when someone makes a breakthrough is one of her greatest joys.

In her life and in her coaching, Ashley draws inspiration from the examples set by her patients, one of whom was happy to tell her about their bucket list. This bucket was not filled with the things they wanted to do but with the memories of a life well-lived that continued to bring joy. They shared that they would reach into their bucket and pull out a memory whenever they felt down.

Ashley Albers, DO

Ashley lives in North Carolina with her pets and enjoys hiking and staying up entirely too late with a good book.

ACKNOWLEDGMENTS

In order to write this book, I had to first become the person who could write it. I had to first do all the work that I've outlined in this book, and I'm grateful to have had a village supporting me.

To all the coaches who have coached me, thank you for helping me to understand my own thoughts.

To all the bosses I've worked for, I've learned something from my time with each of you, and I am grateful.

To Lin, Dustin, Rhianon, and the entire team at AFGO Media & Publishing, wow. You've worked a very special magic here, and I could not have written this book without you. Thank you.

To Mom and Dad, the best supporters anyone could have imagined. Thank you for always being there, especially when I chose to leave what looked like a perfectly wonderful job.

To Lesley, for showing me what's possible and being a beautiful example of what it means to live free. I can't wait to read your next book.

LIVING FREE

How to Stop Living Your Life According to Other People's Expectations

Ashley Albers, DO

To learn more about the **Living Free Framework,** visit: www.livingfreeframework.com

Published by AFGO Press

AFGO Press is a division of AFGO Media and Publishing, whose mission is to support women in building their own businesses.

www.AFGOmedia.com

Made in the USA
Coppell, TX
30 June 2024

34082983R00049